MATH IN OUR WORLD

DOUBLES FUN
ON THE FARM

By Joan Freese

Reading consultant: Susan Nations, M.Ed.,
author/literacy coach/consultant in literacy development
Math consultant: Rhea Stewart, M.A., mathematics content specialist

WEEKLY READER
PUBLISHING

Please visit our web site at www.garethstevens.com
For a free color catalog describing our list of high-quality books,
call 1-800-542-2595 (USA) or 1-800-387-3178 (Canada). Our fax: 1-877-542-2596

Library of Congress Cataloging-in-Publication Data

Freese, Joan.
  Doubles fun on the farm / Joan Freese.
      p. cm. — (Math in our world. Level 2)
    ISBN-13: 978-0-8368-9002-0 (lib. bdg.)
    ISBN-10: 0-8368-9002-7 (lib. bdg.)
    ISBN-13: 978-0-8368-9011-2 (softcover)
    ISBN-10: 0-8368-9011-6 (softcover)
    1. Arithmetic—Juvenile literature. 2. Addition—Juvenile
literature. I. Title.
QA115.F743 2008
513—dc22   2007033379

This edition first published in 2008 by
Weekly Reader® Books
An Imprint of Gareth Stevens Publishing
1 Reader's Digest Road
Pleasantville, NY 10570-7000 USA

Senior Editor: Brian Fitzgerald
Creative Director: Lisa Donovan
Graphic Designer: Alexandria Davis

Photo credits: cover & title page Getty Images; pp. 5, 8, 10, 11, 12, 14, 15, 17, 18, 19, 20, 21, 23,
Russell Pickering; p. 7 National Biological Information Infrastructure; p. 9 © Pinto/zefa/Corbis;
p. 13 © Josh Westrich/zefa/Corbis.

Printed in the United States of America

1 2 3 4 5 6 7 8 9 10 09 08 07

TABLE OF CONTENTS

Words that appear in the glossary are printed in
boldface type the first time they occur in the text.

Chapter 1:
To the Farm

Max lives in the city. He plans to visit his cousin. Her name is Sara. Sara lives on a farm.

Max loves to go to the farm. He visits often.
He likes to play with Sara. He has so much fun.

Chapter 2:
Finding Doubles at the Farm

Max's dad takes him to Sara's house.
Max is excited. "Hello, Sara!" he shouts.
"Hi, Max!" Sara says. Just then Max
sees a bird.

$$1 + 1 = 2$$

Sara spies another bird. "1 bird **plus** 1 bird **equals** 2 birds," she says. "That is a **double!** A double is when you **add** two numbers that are the same."

Sara has 2 dogs. They like to run. They like to play. Sara and Max play fetch with them. Max thinks about doubles.

$$2 + 2 = 4$$

"I get it," he says. "Each dog has 2 ears.
2 dog ears plus 2 dog ears equals 4 dog
ears. That is a double, too."

Sara and Max like playing outdoors.
Being outside makes them hungry. Soon
it is snack time. Sara's mom brings them
something to eat.

3 + 3 = 6

The cousins have crackers for a snack.
Sara takes 3 crackers. Max also takes
3 crackers. They have 6 crackers in all.
A double again!

Now the cousins go for a walk. Sara's mom goes, too. They hunt for four-leaf clovers. The clover plants are in the grass.

$$4 + 4 = 8$$

Sara looks and looks. She finds 2 plants.
Each has 4 leaves. 4 leaves and 4 leaves
make 8 leaves. Another double!

Max and Sara head to the stream. The
stream is on Sara's farm. They take off
their shoes. They wade in the water.

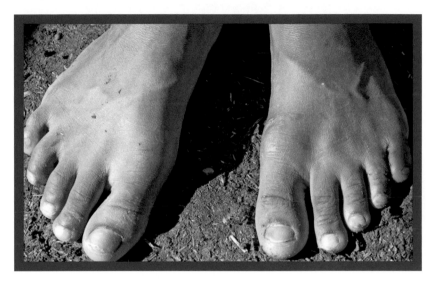

5 + 5 = 10

"Look, my toes are a double!" Max says.

"I have 5 toes on each foot."

Sara looks at her toes. "I do, too," she says.

Chapter 3:
More Doubles Fun

Later, Sara shows Max the garden. Beans and corn grow there. Max likes to eat corn. Other food grows in the garden, too.

$$6 + 6 = 12$$

Sara likes carrots best. She pulls 6 carrots from the ground. Max pulls out 6 carrots, too. They take 12 carrots to Sara's mom.

Next the cousins visit the chickens. Max
and Sara each find a basket. They fill their
baskets with eggs.

$$7 + 7 = 14$$

Sara has 7 eggs in her basket. Max counts out 7 eggs, too. More doubles fun!

Sara and Max walk to the house. Sara sees two spiders. The spiders are making webs. "Look, a spider city!" says Sara.

$$8 + 8 = 16$$

Sara and Max look again. Each spider
has 8 legs. Max thinks about doubles.
"8 legs and 8 more legs makes 16 legs in all!"

Chapter 4:
One Last Double

It is almost time for Max to go home.
The cousins rest near some trees. The
branches hold many apples.

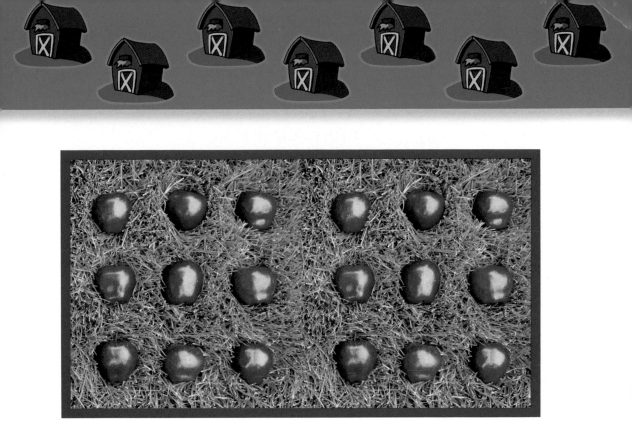

$$9 + 9 = 18$$

Max picks 9 apples. Sara picks 9 apples, too. Max will bring all 18 apples home. They will remind him of the doubles fun today.

Glossary

add: to join 2 or more numbers

doubles: an addition fact in which both numbers being added are the same. 8 + 8 = 16 is a doubles fact.

equals: has the same amount or value

plus: added to

About the Author

Joan Freese has written extensively for children on nonfiction topics from hip-hop dance to hands-on science projects. She lives with her family in Minneapolis, Minnesota.